Jim Elliff

The Eaglet

ED D. KLEIMAN'S
SMALL CLOUD MINISTRIES
www.praybold.org

Illustrated by Caffy Whitney

ISBN: 978-0-9745253-5-8

For copies of *The Eaglet* and information regarding
other materials for children and adults, contact:

Christian Communicators Worldwide (CCW)
201 Main, Suite 3
Parkville, MO 64152

Or visit the CCW website at www.CCWonline.org

Illustrations by Caffy Whitney
Layout and design by Thomas A. Jones

The Eaglet

by Jim Elliff

It is not so surprising that an eaglet would want to fly. This eaglet certainly did. He lived with his mother and father on the top branch of the highest tree on Clear View Peak. This majestic old tree almost touched the clouds as it strained upward from the overhanging ledge. Two sheer cliffs looming up on each side formed a massive gorge called Certain Death.

Every day the frail eaglet watched his stately mother stretch out her eight feet of wings over Certain Death Gorge. Spiraling down, down, down, she was soon only a swirling speck below. There in the fast-running river she would catch the fish the eaglet would eat with her in their nest above.

Oh how he wanted to fly! And if it were not for his father's command, he would do so right this minute.

At his birth, his father swept into the nest with an alarming message. He leaned over into the eaglet's surprised little face and sternly warned, "The day you fly is the day you die!"

To obey would be for his own good, his mother reminded him—it would save his life. And day by day, the mother warned him of his father's words before she spread out her wings to fly again.

But still the eaglet wanted to fly.

One day, after gazing a long time at his mother's silent flight on the wind, he found his own wings slowly stretching out.

Before he knew it, he was on tiptoe prancing around the edge of the nest, pretending to soar through the air!

Suddenly he lost his footing and almost fell! Catching himself, he quickly pulled in his wings and shook his fuzzy head. He remembered again those awful words from his father, "The day you fly is the day you die!"

But as he looked over the edge of the nest, he wondered again just what it would be like to ride the wind.

"Why is it that I want to do what I should not do?" mused the eaglet while resting his head over the lip of the nest. "Perhaps my father is only trying to make life miserable for me."

And then an idea entered his mind which he should never have thought.

"I am big enough to do what I want!" he said to himself. "I will die if I don't fly!" So, foolishly and much too quickly, the eaglet walked up to the edge of the nest, lifted his wings and . . . *jumped!*

It took only a second of time for the eaglet to know he had done the wrong thing. His scrawny wings did not have large feathers or strong muscles and could not catch the waves of wind or push against the air to stop his fall. Soon the rushing air forced his wings up beside his face. His feet came right along beside them, and he went down like a stone.

He was doomed. Faster and faster he went, passing ledge after ledge. He was plummeting to his death below. And worst of all, he could do nothing about it.

He could, of course, try to forget what he was about to experience and simply enjoy the breath-taking beauty of the mountain on the way down. But this was impossible. Try as he might, the alarming thought of dying would not leave him.

"I will die. It was my choice," he thought. "I did what I wanted and will get what my father promised. There is no joy in this freedom of mine, only sorrow and death. I have disobeyed and am ruined forever. I hate my sin! **This is the day I fly and the day I die!**"

He knew now that his only help must come from someone other than himself. He needed a rescuer. He knew of only one who could actually do that. Oh how he would willingly obey if only his father would come to help him now!

In his fear and desperation he let out a scream: **"H-E-L-P!"**
The word echoed back and forth on the walls of the deep
gorge, **"HELP! HELP! HELP! HELP!"**

And then, just before reaching the bottom of Certain
Death Gorge, he heard a *"swoosh!"*

Feeling the piercing pain of talons in his back, his head
jerked forward as he stopped in midair. Immediately his
downward motion was reversed. It was his father! At just
the right moment, the very one he had disobeyed had come
to his rescue.

His father's powerful wings pumped mightily, upward,
upward, upward. The little eaglet's eyes were full of amaze-
ment and tears. The teardrops fell to the river below, tears
of thankfulness and love. Soon the one deserving to die
would be safe in the nest above.

A Lesson of Life and Death

Did you know that *you* are just like that eaglet? The Bible tells us that we have all chosen to do what we want to do rather than what the *Father* says we must do. Our disobedience is called sin. Over and over again we sin against God. And God has warned us that the person who sins will die!

It is an awful death the sinner dies. The eaglet was going to die at the bottom of Certain Death Gorge, do you remember? Yet the sinner's death is far worse than this. Not only will the sinner's *body* die one day, but his *soul* as well will be sent forever to a place called hell. It is hard to explain how bad hell is. Jesus said it was a place of torment and pain, full of sorrow and distress. It is a living death. And, saddest of all, the people who go to hell will never get out. Hell is forever.

Just like the eaglet, you have disobeyed the Father. And you deserve to go to hell. God Himself must send you there, for He is just. This is the truth—Jesus taught it Himself.

But listen to what else the Bible says: "For when we were still without strength, in due time Christ died for the ungodly. . . . God demonstrates His own love toward us, in that while we were still sinners, Christ died for us" (Romans 5:6, 8).

Just as the eaglet was powerless to help himself while falling to his death, so we are powerless to help ourselves to safety from hell. But Christ died to take on Himself the penalty from God for the sins of *all* those who will believe. We do not have to die for them ourselves! What an act of love this was! And to prove beyond any question that He conquered the power of sin and death, He rose from the dead after three days. He is alive today!

The Bible says that Christ will save you from this awful place called hell if you will come to him. But how should you do that? The Bible says you must come by *repentance* and *faith*.

Do you remember what the eaglet said on the way down? "I will die. It was my choice. I did what I wanted and will get what my father promised. There is no joy in this freedom of mine, only sorrow and death. I have disobeyed and I am ruined forever. I hate my sin! This is the day I fly *and* the day I die!" He was repenting of his disobedience. Repentance is a change of mind. Repentance says, "I hate what I once loved, and I love what I once hated."

Do you hate your sin? Do you have a desire to be changed by God? Do you want to be obedient if God gives you the ability? Do you want Christ to be the Lord of your life?

Faith is putting your confidence in Christ to save you from your life of sin and the hell you deserve. The eaglet had no one he could trust but his father. He looked to his father alone for help. And you have no hope but Christ. He died for sinners like you. In fact, He does *everything* to save the one who comes to Him. Each believer will someday find that even the desire to turn to Him was a gift from Him.

God says all who repent and believe (have faith) in Christ, and in what He has done on the cross, will receive the gift of eternal life. This means that when they die, they will go to heaven; and while they live here, they will know, love, and serve Christ as their true Master and Savior.

Can you understand why the eaglet's tears flowed after he was rescued? He was changed from one who hated to obey to one who loved to obey, and he was now safe in the grasp of his father, soon to be placed in the nest above.

How much more thankful should a believer be! God has given him the ability to repent and trust in Christ for forgiveness of his sins as well as life with Him in heaven.

There is a way, the Bible says, that seems right, but ends in death. The end of a life of disobeying God is Certain Death. But the gift of God is eternal life in Christ Jesus for all who believe (trust) in Him. You must do so or you will spend an eternity in hell. God says it. It is true.

Have you repented and trusted in Christ? Pray that you might *know* whether or not you have become His child. If you have repented and believed, you will not be perfect, but you will be a changed person and a true Christian.

And don't forget to be as thankful as the eaglet. Your salvation is far more amazing than his.

Remember—

1. You have sinned against a holy God. (Romans 3:10-12, 23; James 2:10)

2. Because of your sin you deserve eternity in hell as God's judgment. (Romans 6:23; Hebrews 9:27)

3. Jesus Christ died on the cross. There He took the punishment sinners deserve for their sin. He then rose from the dead, conquering sin and death. (John 10:11; Romans 5:8)

4. You must repent and believe. Place your full trust in Christ as your only Savior from sin and hell. He must be the new Master of your life. (Luke 13:3; Acts 16:29-31; Ephesians 2:8-9)

5. You can be sure of your salvation if you keep on trusting in Christ and live as a true Christian. (Matthew 7:21-23; John 10:27-30)

For God so loved

the world that He gave

His only begotten Son,

that whoever believes in Him

should not perish but

have everlasting life.

John 3:16

Christian Communicators Worldwide

CCW is a ministry based in Parkville, Missouri, a "river-stop" town in the Northland of the greater Kansas City area. We enjoy this quaint town with its beautiful park, interesting shops and eateries, and the stately Park University that overlooks it all. The meandering Missouri River, navigated by Lewis and Clark on their expedition, runs along the south end of the town. Independence, Missouri, the starting place for the Oregon and Santa Fe trails, is not far from Parkville. There is a lot of history here at "the beginning of the Westward advance."

Like those who explored and settled the western regions of the United States, CCW is also on a mission—to extend the message of Christ as far as God will allow. We do that through our websites (see next page) and through the speaking ministry of our founder, Jim Elliff. We also do this through Jim's writing ministry and that of his assistants, Daryl Wingerd and Susan Verstraete. CCW publishes books and booklets, offered by us and by other booksellers. Tens of thousands of pieces of free literature have also been distributed, both here and overseas.

Please visit our web sites:

www.CCWonline.org

This is our main site, with numerous articles, ministry tools, audio messages, and information about ordering our publications.

www.WaytoGod.org

This site contains articles and audio designed to guide interested people into a relationship with Jesus Christ. Here we also answer questions from inquirers.

www.BulletinInserts.org

This site provides timely and instructive bulletin inserts, handouts, and tracts. We offer free, downloadable inserts (also available in A4) for every Sunday of the year.